Tectonic Plates
Are on the Move

By NADIA HIGGINS
Illustrations by JIA LIU
Music by DEAN JONES

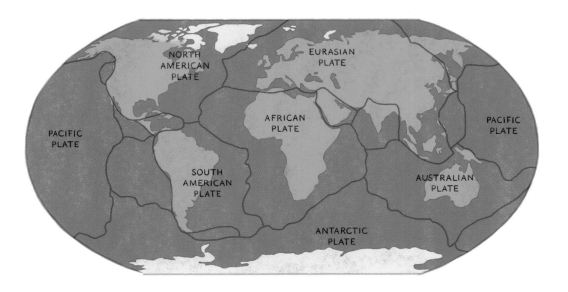

CANTATA
LEARNING

WWW.CANTATALEARNING.COM

CANTATA LEARNING

Published by Cantata Learning
1710 Roe Crest Drive
North Mankato, MN 56003
www.cantatalearning.com

Library of Congress Cataloging-in-Publication Data
Names: Higgins, Nadia, author. | Liu, Jia (Illustrator), illustrator. |
   Jones, Dean, 1966– composer.
Title: Tectonic plates are on the move / by Nadia Higgins ; illustrated by
   Jia Liu ; music by Dean Jones.
Description: North Mankato, MN : Cantata Learning, [2018] | Series: What
   shapes our Earth? | Audience: Ages 6–9. | Audience: K to grade 3. |
   Includes lyrics and sheet music. | Includes bibliographical references.
Identifiers: LCCN 2017017552 (print) | LCCN 2017037927 (ebook) | ISBN
   9781684101733 (ebook) | ISBN 9781684101443 (hardcover : alk. paper)
Subjects: LCSH: Plate tectonics--Juvenile literature. | Children's songs,
   English.
Classification: LCC QE511.4 (ebook) | LCC QE511.4 .H54 2018 (print) | DDC
   551.1/36--dc23
LC record available at https://lccn.loc.gov/2017017552

Book design and art direction, Tim Palin Creative
Editorial direction, Kellie M. Hultgren
Music direction, Elizabeth Draper
Music arranged and produced by Dean Jones

Printed in the United States of America in North Mankato, Minnesota.
122017   0378CGS18

ACCESS THE MUSIC!

SCAN CODE WITH MOBILE APP

CANTATALEARNING.COM

TIPS TO SUPPORT LITERACY AT HOME

WHY READING AND SINGING WITH YOUR CHILD IS SO IMPORTANT

Daily reading with your child leads to increased academic achievement. Music and songs, specifically rhyming songs, are a fun and easy way to build early literacy and language development. Music skills correlate significantly with both phonological awareness and reading development. Singing helps build vocabulary and speech development. And reading and appreciating music together is a wonderful way to strengthen your relationship.

READ AND SING EVERY DAY!

TIPS FOR USING CANTATA LEARNING BOOKS AND SONGS DURING YOUR DAILY STORY TIME

1. As you sing and read, point out the different words on the page that rhyme. Suggest other words that rhyme.

2. Memorize simple rhymes such as Itsy Bitsy Spider and sing them together. This encourages comprehension skills and early literacy skills.

3. Use the questions in the back of each book to guide your singing and storytelling.

4. Read the included sheet music with your child while you listen to the song. How do the music notes correlate to the words of the song?

5. Sing along on the go and at home. Access music by scanning the QR code on each Cantata book. You can also stream or download the music for free to your computer, smartphone, or mobile device.

Devoting time to daily reading shows that you are available for your child. Together, you are building language, literacy, and listening skills.

Have fun reading and singing!

Did you know you are never *really* standing still? Way down under your feet, the ground is always moving. Giant pieces called **tectonic plates** slowly slide past each other. They crash and drift apart. Over time, their motion makes big changes on our planet.

Turn the page. Sing along to this Earth-changing song!

Earth has layers like a sandwich.
A thin **crust** forms the very top.

CRUST —

Under land and ocean floors,
it slides around on melted rock.

MANTLE

CORE

Earth's crust is made of giant pieces
slowly shifting under your shoes.

They grind. They crash.
 They pull apart.
Tectonic plates are
 on the move.

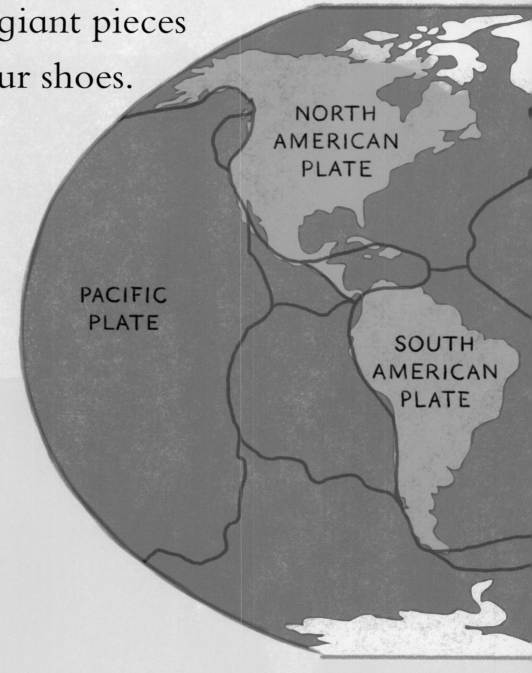

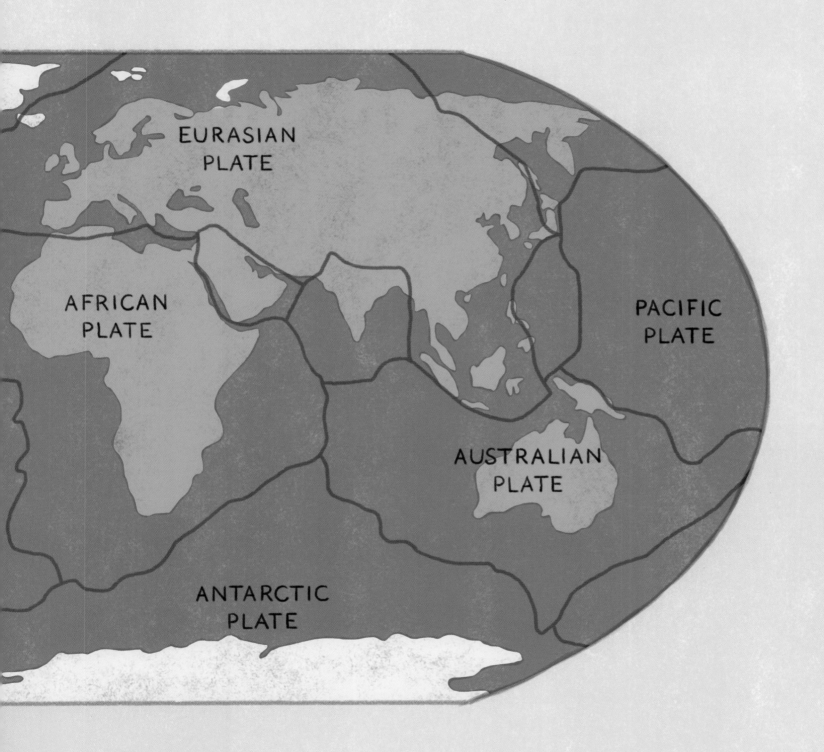

Tectonic plates slide past each other.
The plates get stuck, and **tension** builds.

All at once, the plates break free
and an earthquake ripples through the hills.

San Andreas Fault

Earth's crust is made of giant pieces slowly shifting under your shoes.

They grind. They crash. They pull apart. Tectonic plates are on the move.

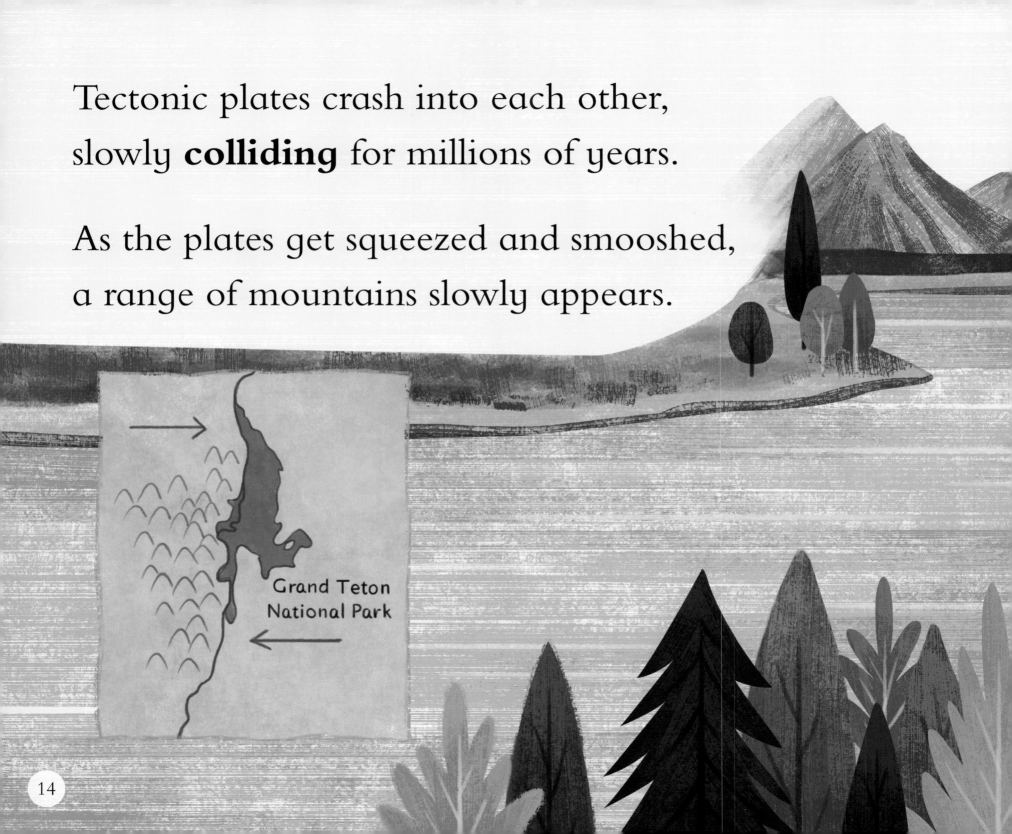

Tectonic plates crash into each other, slowly **colliding** for millions of years.

As the plates get squeezed and smooshed, a range of mountains slowly appears.

Grand Teton
National Park

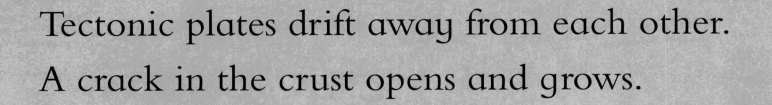

Tectonic plates drift away from each other.
A crack in the crust opens and grows.

Hot melted rock comes bubbling up,
until out from a volcano the **lava** flows.

Move your hands like tectonic plates.
Slide them. Grind them. Feel the ground shake.

Clap them together. Mountains will grow.
Pull them apart. Volcanoes flow.

Earth's crust is made of giant pieces
slowly shifting under your shoes.

They grind. They crash. They pull apart.
Tectonic plates are on the move.

SONG LYRICS
Tectonic Plates Are On the Move

Earth has layers like a sandwich.
A thin crust forms on the very top.
Under land and ocean floors,
it slides around on melted rock.

Earth's crust is made of giant pieces
slowly shifting under your shoes.
They grind. They crash. They pull apart.
Tectonic plates are on the move.

Tectonic plates slide past each other.
The plates get stuck, and tension builds.
All at once, the plates break free
and an earthquake ripples through the hills.

Earth's crust is made of giant pieces
slowly shifting under your shoes.
They grind. They crash. They pull apart.
Tectonic plates are on the move.

Tectonic plates crash into each other,
slowly colliding for millions of years.
As the plates get squeezed and smooshed,
a range of mountains slowly appears.

Tectonic plates drift away from each other.
A crack in the crust opens and grows.
Hot melted rock comes bubbling up,
until out from a volcano the lava flows.

Move your hands like tectonic plates.
Slide them. Grind them. Feel the ground shake.
Clap them together. Mountains will grow.
Pull them apart. Volcanoes flow.

Earth's crust is made of giant pieces
slowly shifting under your shoes.
They grind. They crash. They pull apart.
Tectonic plates are on the move.

Tectonic Plates Are On the Move

Tango Pop
Dean Jones

Verse

1. Earth has lay - ers like a sand - wich. A thin crust forms on the ver - y top. Un-der land and o-cean floors, it slides a-round on melt-ed rock.

Chorus 1, 2, 4

Earth's crust is made of gi - ant piec - es slow-ly shift - ing un - der your shoes. They grind. They crash. They pull a - part.

Tec - ton - ic plates are on the move.

Verse 2
Tectonic plates slide past each other.
The plates get stuck, and tension builds.
All at once, the plates break free
and an earthquake ripples through the hills.

Chorus

Verse 3
Tectonic plates crash into each other,
slowly colliding for millions of years.
As the plates get squeezed and smooshed,
a range of mountains slowly appears.

Chorus 3

Tec - ton - ic plates drift a - way from each oth - er. A crack in the crust o - pens and grows. Hot melt - ed rock

comes bub - bl - ing up, un - til out from a vol-ca - no the la - va flows.

Verse 4
Move your hands like tectonic plates.
Slide them. Grind them. Feel the ground shake.
Clap them together. Mountains will grow.
Pull them apart. Volcanoes flow.

Chorus

GLOSSARY

colliding—crashing into something

crust—the top layer of Earth, made up of land and ocean floors

lava—hot, melted rock that flows out of volcanoes

tectonic plates—giant pieces of Earth's crust

tension—stress that builds up inside something, such as rocks

GUIDED READING ACTIVITIES

1. Tectonic plates move about 1 to 4 inches (2.5 to 10 cm) a year. How much did you grow last year? Did you grow faster or slower than a tectonic plate moves?

2. More than 200 million years ago, Earth had had just one giant continent called Pangaea. Tectonic plates pushed Pangaea apart. With an adult's help, find a map of Pangaea.

3. Have you ever felt an earthquake? Has a family member? Share your story or listen to theirs. What happened? What did it feel like?

TO LEARN MORE

Furgang, Kathy. *Everything Volcanoes and Earthquakes.* Washington, DC: National Geographic, 2013.

Oxlade, Chris. *Mountains.* Chicago: Heinemann Library, 2014.

Winchester, Simon. *When the Earth Shakes: Earthquakes, Volcanoes, and Tsunamis.* New York: Viking, 2015.